SELECTED DECLARATIONS
OF DEPENDENCE

Books by Harry Mathews

FICTION

The Conversions (Random House, 1962)
Tlooth (Doubleday, 1966)
The Sinking of the Odradek Stadium (Harper & Row, 1975)
Selected Declarations of Dependence (Z Press, 1977;
Sun & Moon Press, 1996)
Country Cooking and Other Stories (Burning Deck, 1980)
Singular Pleasures (The Grenfell Press, 1988;
Dalkey Archive Press, 1993)
Cigarettes (Weidenfeld & Nicolson, 1988)
20 Lines a Day (Dalkey Archive, 1988)
The Journalist (David Godine, 1994)

POETRY

The Ring (Julliard, 1961)
The Planisphere (Burning Deck, 1974)
Trial Impressions (Burning Deck, 1977)
Armenian Papers: Poems 1954–1984
(Princeton University Press, 1987)
Out of Bounds (Burning Deck, 1989)

ESSAYS

The Orchard (Bamberger Books, 1988)
Immeasurable Distances (The Lapis Press, 1991)

Harry Mathews

Selected Declarations
of Dependence

with Illustrations by Alex Katz
and a Foreword by the Author

SUN &
MOON

CLASSICS

128

SUN & MOON PRESS

LOS ANGELES • 1996

Sun & Moon Press
A Program of The Contemporary Arts Educational Project, Inc.
a nonprofit corporation
6026 Wilshire Boulevard, Los Angeles, California 90036

This edition first published in paperback in 1996 by Sun & Moon Press
10 9 8 7 6 5 4 3 2 1
FIRST SUN & MOON PRESS EDITION
©1977 by Harry Mathews
Foreword ©1996 by Harry Mathews
Illustrations ©1996, 1977 by Alex Katz
Biographical material ©1996 by Sun & Moon Press
All rights reserved

Originally published by Z Press (Calais, Vermont) in 1977.

This book was made possible, in part, through an operational grant from the
Andrew W. Mellon Foundation and through contributions to
The Contemporary Arts Educational Project, Inc.,
a nonprofit corporation

Cover: *Three British Soldiers*, by Alex Katz
Reprinted by permission of the artist.
Design: Katie Messborn
Typography: Guy Bennett

LIBRARY OF CONGRESS CATALOGING IN PUBLICATION DATA
Mathews, Harry [1930]
Selected Declarations of Dependence
p. cm — (Sun & Moon Classics: 128)
ISBN: 1-55713-234-8
1. Title. 11. Series.
811'.54—dc20

Printed in the United States of America on acid-free paper.

Contents

Where are the shows of yesteryear?
—VENETIAN PROVERB

for JOHN ASHBERY

Foreword

Selected Declarations of Dependence is based on a set of forty-six familiar proverbs, used and abused in various ways:

The forty-six proverbs provide the entire vocabulary of the opening story, "Their Words, For You."

The sections called "Perverbs and Paraphrases" explore the narrative implications of the crossed proverb or "perverb".

(Two suitable proverbs yield two perverbs—for example, "All roads lead to Rome" and "A rolling stone gathers no moss" supply, when crossed, the perverbs "All roads gather no moss" and "A rolling stone leads to Rome.") The perverbs that gave rise to the so-called paraphrases have been listed randomly in order to leave the pleasure of making appropriate connections to the reader.

The remaining uses of proverbs and perverbs are pretty much self-evident. If you know "The House that Jack Built," you will see why Jack is the one to remind the King of Karactika of certain truths. The "Sorites" bows to Lewis Carroll's hilarious demonstration of the form, to a more reasonable end, in his *Symbolic Logic*.

Lans, December 26, 1989

THEIR WORDS, FOR YOU

I

Another morning, another egg. The sky was up early. It had rained all night: to you and me sleeping, the storm was a delight. In the east, morning clouds are building a kingdom of red and silver. Time for you to get up! Come into the kingdom of morning delight and come as king! Come into the omelet of morning delight, and come as egg!

You can't make an omelet without breaking half a dozen of the other. Take six eggs...Eggs are things—eggs *were* things: have an omelet. Have a little bread with it too. Cat! Come on Cat, you old dog, have a little bread till it's bone time.

You're looking good today. What of going down the road to the port? No—you propose old-stone-gathering at the water side, and going into the water when the tide comes in.

You go with me down fences that teach the intentions of the men that dispose of the grass. A horse waits at a fence; another rolls on the grass, breaking wind. (Good for the horse—one should break wind when one has to, putting it off does no good.) At the side of the road dead grass is burning, old sticks and grass, burning silver in the morning. The road is a delight, with water on one side, oaks and grass on the other; and the grass leads away to another water. In the oaks you once gathered bird's eggs from moss.

From the road you can see the port, the old port paved with stones, paved with bones. Sailors gather in it at night, gathering on the night side of the port looking for the tricks and stitches of love.

God disposes
  Red sky at night,
Man proposes
  Sailor's delight

When the tide is coming in, sailors can drink and sleep. In the morning all leave on the early tide. Not all: a few go on sleeping.

"All roads lead to rooms"
——IRISH PROVERB

All roads lead to good intentions;
East is east and west is west, and God disposes;
Time and tide in a storm.
All roads, sailor's delight.
(Many are called, sailors take warning:
All roads wait for no man.)

All roads are soon parted.
East is east and west is west: twice shy.
Time and tide bury their dead.
A rolling stone, sailor's delight.
"Any port"——sailors take warning:
All roads are another man's poison.

All roads take the hindmost,
East is east and west is west and few are chosen,
Time and tide are soon parted,
The devil takes sailors' delight.
Once burned, sailors take warning:
All roads bury their dead.

All roads have a silver lining;
East is east and west is west in a storm;
Time and tide are as good as a mile.
East is east and west is west—sailor's delight.
(East is east and west is west, sailors take warning!)
All roads are worth two in the bush.

II

Men that had been sailors came to be men of roads and grass. A dozen men proposed to build the roads. Others disposed the fences. Men broke stones to pave and build. The men break new bread and drink new water, and pour new water over their hands.

Not all took to the new kingdom (one with no king). Water can look good even to a one-eyed sailor—"a sailor with no love of the water is an unlucky man"—and sailors that had the love went off on new tides. Soon a port was built—built, it has been taught, with the bones of dead men, dead sailors. Soon the stones of the port looked green with moss, and silver with gatherings of birds.

Other sailors took to building, and making things, and being men of oaks and grass, and horse men. "A sailor on a horse had better be lucky"—but half a dozen times will teach even unlucky men, when their intentions are mighty. From east to west the grasses were gathered, and stone and oak were built up to the sky—no, not to the sky: but a new kingdom was made.

You go with me into a break in the fence, on which suckers are growing. On the other side a man is teaching a horse, "breaking" him. The horse—red, shy, and mighty—is looking into the wind. The man is looking away from the wind—he is looking at the horse. He leads him with one hand, having a stick in the other.

You led me to the water. The tide was down, leaving many stones to look at, green and red, with tide water lying in the lining of the stones. Birds that had waited when the tide was in have gathered at the water's side, downwind.

You go into the water. But it's no time for stone gathering. From the water to the west a new wind is blowing, and to the west a storm is building, coming with the wind. All at once it's time to go away. In a storm it is the fool that takes to the water.

Getting to the road you called to me, "It's going to rain cats and dogs!" And soon the wind pours down the waters it has gathered.

In the oaks by the side of the road, old men had been playing cards on the grass. When the storm broke, other men left off building and came to play with the old men, waiting till the storm blew on. One old man lay sleeping. You waited with me a little away from the men playing and sleeping: "Mighty oaks in a storm."

It was raining on every side. The storm paved the sky with stone.

Let it rain; let the wind blow. Down kingdoms of grass and stone the wind teaches you: wait. Wait, and sleep. The wind will blow, the night will come, the storm will break. We shall go into the night to sleep, the night in which, as in words, mouths meet.

> *Every cloud blows no good.*
>> You can't make an omelet in a storm.
>> *Red sky at morning waits for no man,*
>> *Time and tide gather no moss.*
> *Every cloud, sailors take warning.*
>> *"It never rains"?—twice shy.*
>> *It's an ill wind that has its day.*
>> East is east and west is west, but it pours.

Every cloud wasn't built in a day.
    All roads in a storm.
    Red sky at night, but God disposes.
    Time and tide have their day.
Every cloud must come down,
    It never rains with good intentions.
    It's an ill wind that's as good as a mile.
    Red sky at night, but it pours.

Every cloud buries its dead.
    The road to Hell in a storm.
    Red sky at night, twice shy.
    Time and tide, sailors take warning.
Every cloud is another man's poison
    (It never rains on the other side of the fence.)
    It's an ill wind that wasn't built in a day.
    All roads, but it pours.

Every cloud gets the worm.
    It's an ill wind in a storm.
    Red sky at night has a silver lining…
    Time and tide take the hindmost,
Every cloud waits for no man:
    It never rains before you leap.
    It's an ill wind that must come down.
    Sticks and stones may break my bones, but it pours.

Every cloud must come down—
    A stitch in time in a storm.
    Red sky at morning, but God disposes:
    Time and tide have a silver lining.
Every cloud is soon parted.
    It never rains—sailor's delight.
    It's an ill wind that waits for no man;
    And man proposes—but it pours.

III

In the night, water poured from the sky, to call up in the morning a new tide of worms—which with the water will make for better grass. The rain went away early, as the east went from silver to silver-and-red. The night was done, and what a night! Not water and a dozen devils could have spoiled it. A night of love: in which you made me come twice, and once in the morning. Don't let the words make you red and shy!

The break of day proposes new things: new bread, for one. Bread makes the morning. Look! in the east, red breadloaf clouds. But the little clouds the wind rolls down the grass look green. The fences look green too: the storm has made old fences new.

Six birds break from a green cloud and go off. Other little birds gather for the bread you'll give. A redbird! Shy birds gather on the even grass, going up and down before coming up to the water to drink and play. Others wait on a fence. And in the bushes wait the cats. As it is, cats can wait for six tomorrows, it won't harm the birds and it won't do the cats any good. As soon as a bird takes in a cat's intention, it leaves the

grass and takes to a bush; in time leaves the bush to take to an oak; and soon a cat is looking down from the green oak....

From early morning every bird has been calling to every other bird, making their intentions mighty: "*My* worms, *my* worms..."

The early bird waits for no man.
The early bird gathers no moss.
 A bird in the hand is soon parted.
The early bird gets what you can do today.
  Red sky at morning gets the worm.

The early bird is soon parted—
The early bird is on the other side of the fence!
 A bird in the hand is twice shy.
The early bird leaves no stone unturned,
  A rolling stone gets the worm.

The early bird is another man's poison.
The early bird from little acorns grows.
 A bird in the hand waits for no man.
Early bird, unlucky in love.
  Sticks and stones get the worm.

The early bird has its day,
The early bird, and half a dozen of the other:
 A bird in the hand is better than no bread.
The early bird is worth two in the bush.
  Time and tide get the worm.

On the other side of the fence, two little dogs are rolling on the grass. Have they been taught to come when called? Look—the dogs are coming without a word from you. Good dogs, that come at once. (But *better* dogs do not come without being called.)

No, it isn't for you. The dogs are going over to look at another man. The one coming down the other side of the fence, the one you've met before. Can't you put him off? Don't let the loaf burn.

Soon two other dogs meet the first two. It's the cook's dogs—lucky dogs to be a cook's! One is waiting to play "get the stick." Good. With a stick one can teach a dog many tricks, when one does it with love.

But when the other dogs came, the cats left, all six. Even one dog can dispose of many a cat; and when dogs gather, cats take the intention to be other than that of burying bones. When one chooses a dog, it is better for the good of one's little kingdom to get a dog that can lie down with a cat and play with it.

You go off to propose things to the other man. Always playing the fool—you, not him: playing the fool is a delight fools cannot have. But every man has a side worth looking at—once.

Another, one-eyed dog has come and is making water on the side of the oak.

for "Fred" *You can't teach an old dog to leave no stone unturned.*
Let every dog lie—
Every dog is another man's poison;
Let sleeping dogs have their day—
Every dog has its good intentions.
Sleeping dogs weren't built in a day.

You can't teach an old dog on the other side of the fence.
Every dog has its new tricks,
Every dog gathers no moss,
Sleeping dogs wait for no man.
Every dog is worth two in the bush:
Leave no sleeping dog unturned.

You can't teach an old dog without breaking eggs.
Every dog waits for no man;
Every dog is soon parted.
Sleeping dogs have a silver lining
(Every dog must come down.)
Never give sleeping dogs an even break.

You can't teach sleeping dogs new tricks.
Every dog takes the hindmost—
Every dog gets the worm.
Never look sleeping dogs in the mouth.
Every dog, take warning:
Sleeping dogs gather no moss.

Waiting for him to go away. The wind has broken up the sky of clouds, it's parting the clouds from the sky. It's an ill wind on the other side of the fence. And him so old! You being with him makes him look old. Does it make me look old? You're going to let the bread burn.

Better bury my words. Better to leave, and burn, and wait for a new day. And on the morning of my lucky night...!

Better? For what? Not for me.

The good, for a dog, is a bone with meat on it. For a cat the good is little, shy dogs, and many mice. The good for mice is no cats, and a left loaf of bread. The good for birds is no cats, and eggs saved from cats and men. For a horse the good is new grass, and other horses, and a few good men. For man the good is no one thing.

For a sailor, the good is even tides, many ports, and half a wind.

For a cook, the good is unburned meat and the delight of other men.

For one king the good is a kingdom without fools; for another, the good is a kingdom all fools.

For Caesar the good is what makes him Caesar.

For a fool the good is other fools. For other men, the good is what makes fools shy.

But for me, the good is you.

IV

In the early morning a lucky worm would go on sleeping. But what worm sleeps? The egg lies waiting to be a better egg; but it is not to be. What good is the intention of an egg? Time and man "spoil" the egg by making it into another thing—a bird, an omelet.

Soon the cat comes in. It looks at the omelet without any delight at all and goes off.

For me too the day is spoiled. You have gone off. You have even gone off without leaving me any bread. It has taken me a little time to gather what an unlucky wind is blowing. You had led me to look to many good days, green and even days that would propose love and all the little delights that love can save

and build into a kingdom—moss, dogs, red eggs....But it is not to be. Every day makes new fools out of old ones, and today has chosen me. Like the eggs, my gifts lie broken and not to be gathered up. Is it "growing old"?

> *A stitch in time,*
> *A bird in the hand,*
> *A silver lining*
> *Wait for no man*

And you can't save an omelet with stitches. You came on all shy with me, when the intention was to take a stick to a dog that had not harmed you. What good are silver words to me when you have as good as left me? Things spoil, burn, and are buried—men for one—and words cannot make the things new.

And to do it for *him*! When you take another man, take a good one—not a fool, not a mouse, not one who plays cards all day. But was it for him that you did it, for him as him? Wasn't it for all the money that's been left him? You shouldn't have given him the time of day, in other times you would have made him get away at once, but you looked at him and drank with him and took gifts from him and soon were disposed to sleep with him. Did you do this for money—for the meat off dead men's bones? One was taught that "a fool and his money spoil the broth": the words were made for you. And today you propose to me not to put you off, to take love from you as it is given. Don't lie to me always! You're not blind to the poison you've poured into my days. What a sucker you take me for! That's not new—no, and you're getting better at it all the time.

You're looking good—as good as always. Have you been down at the water side? The wind's burned you—that red mouth. You're going? It's not even six.—Have a good time. Don't take my words to you for ill intentions. My words aren't stones to harm you but fences to make you not harm me. Things will go better for me soon: any tomorrow is better than none, and half a loaf (being with you from time to time)—half a loaf is better than no silver lining.

Come soon—will you come tomorrow and look at my new cards?

Come as soon as you can.

Gone. Day, night: time and tide spoil the broth. You lay down once in the bushes with me. Are you lying down with him, in the bushes on the other side of the road?—Go look? Gathering words one can look at, bush words—"…Give it…take it…" Let it be.

Time has no intentions. It "never sleeps" but it is always sleeping. It will bury tomorrow as it has buried today, without delight, without love. It is not lucky and not unlucky, it does no good and no ill, it is blind and not blind (can it look?), it is old and not old (it never can "be" at all), it is not little and not mighty: but things grow, things spoil, things break, things are built, things are given, things are saved, things are buried, things sleep—and "time" renders the doing and the things done, in nights and days.

<dd>Dante</dd>

From me one goes into the burning kingdom;
From me one goes into the poison of all tomorrows;
From me one goes to meet men left for dead.
To give good to the good, and ill to the ill, led the mighty one who
made me:
Made me God's mighty Gift,
The Word that gathers all things, and the Love that has no better.
Till me were no things made
But things without time, and time is without me.
Leave all chosen intentions of days to come, you that come in.

V

Words came from you in the morning. One word on the little
card said "Rome"—a word that buried my day. You're going to
Rome with him. The word made me look up at you as you
went away down the road, without having waited for me to
come down. It made me give up.

Another gift, and what a gift! Soon you will have met him
a dozen times—dozens of times. And every time money is
rained on you. Do you play cards? You make money playing
cards. Do you look at a horse with love? The horse is gotten
for you. And soon Rome: an intention that, in the words you
left me, is a "thing of delight"—thing, thing! Hasn't it been
taught him that a dozen gifts spoil one?

You never proposed to me to go away with you. But having
money and things is not my gift, and it never will be, no. My
gifts to you were little, but given with love. My gifts were
few—too few. Half a loaf, unlucky in love.

You never proposed to me to go away, and you aren't doing it today. Couldn't you have done it and left it to me to put off my leaving with you? (With you and him.) A little gift to *me*. You wouldn't have had to wait for my "no"—even to one as blind as me, it's no trick to get what's on the cards.

> *When in Rome*
> > *Few are chosen,*
> *Six of one*
> > *Are another man's poison*

Even one of one. "Too many cooks spoil the bird in the hand," no? And at any time, with you or without you, Rome is not my thing. If one man's meat is the things that are Caesar's, the man must be him and not me.

"Rome is another man's poison"
—BYZANTINE PROVERB

Sticks and stones may break my bones, but words lead to Rome:
"Red sky at night, do as the Romans do—
Rome wasn't built in a storm...."
When in Rome, gather no moss:
All silver linings lead to Rome.
Lucky at cards, do as the Romans do,
Render unto Caesar, and "God disposes."
The grass is always greener when it leads to Rome.
When in Rome, do as the gift horses do.
When in Rome, sailor's delight.
All roads lead to the things which are Caesar's.
The early bird gets the things which are Caesar's.

The early bird leads to Rome.
When the cat's away, do as the Romans do.
Rome wasn't built from little acorns.
When in Rome, words will never harm me.
All gift horses lead to Rome:
Render unto Caesar as the Romans do.
Render unto Caesar before you leap—
A stitch in time leads to Rome!
East is east, and west is west, and do as the Romans do.
When in Rome, twice shy:
Never give a sucker the things which are Caesar's.
Never put off till tomorrow the things which are Caesar's.

Any port leads to Rome.
All roads do as the Romans do.
(Rome wasn't built on the other side of the fence.)
When in Rome, take it with you.
Time and tide lead to Rome,
Many are called; but do as the Romans do.
Render unto Caesar on the other side of the fence.
Man proposes, and leads to Rome
—Once burned, do as the Romans do.
When in Rome, the one-eyed man is king . . .
Man proposes the things which are Caesar's
—The devil take the things which are Caesar's!

It's an ill wind that leads to Rome.
Time and tide do as the Romans do,
Rome wasn't built but it poured.
When in Rome, sailors take warning:
Every cloud leads to Rome.
Red sky at morning, do as the Romans do,
Render unto Caesar in a storm.
A fool and his money lead to Rome.
Let sleeping dogs do as the Romans do.
When in Rome, wait for no man—
A miss is as good as the things which are Caesar's.
Every dog has the things which are Caesar's.

Many are called, but few lead to Rome.
In the kingdom of the blind, do as the Romans do.
(Rome wasn't built as the Romans do.)
When in Rome, unlucky in love.
A rolling stone leads to Rome.
Sticks and stones do as the Romans do.
Render unto Caesar—but words will never harm me.
The road to Hell leads to Rome:
Many are called but do as the Romans do.
(When in Rome, bury their dead.)
A fool and his money are the things which are Caesar's.
Half a loaf is better than the things which are Caesar's.

Every dog leads to Rome.
Look before you do as the Romans do:
Rome wasn't built with a silver lining.
When in Rome, take the hindmost.
Sticks and stones lead to Rome,
A fool and his money do as the Romans do,
Render unto Caesar; but few are chosen.
Let the dead lead to Rome;
Let the dead do as the Romans do.
When in Rome, few are chosen.
Sticks and stones may break the things which are Caesar's.
Let the dead bury the things which are Caesar's.

And soon *you'll* be rolling down to Rome. Have a good
time, go east, go west, but——when in Rome, God disposes!
And will dispose of him, could be, with him as old as an oak.
No, my days aren't that lucky; but the unturned card is always
the sucker's delight.

VI

In the red and silver morning a dead day breaks. New words
from you to teach me that, once looked on by you as a king
(even too mighty a one, which harms me)——once a king, but
broken to a stone, a stick, to be buried in parted days as a dead
bird or mouse is buried in the grass. The words that came to
you from me in the night you call the poison of love gone
dead——you take me to have left the kingdom that was my king-
dom with you and to have gone blind, to have grown spoiled——
a man spoiled as meat is spoiled——

Shakespeare "The ones that have the gift to harm and will do none,
that do not do the things which others always look at,
that, disposing others, are as stone,
not disposed any way, without love, shy of delight,
are the men that must be left the gifts of God,
and must gather the moneys of the kingdom of days and not let
    them be parted,
that are kings of their looking,
and others but ones that gather and dispose of their mighty gifts.
Bushes grow things that are delights to the days of green
(delights that are blind to all things but their coming and going)
but if a delight with ill poison meets,
any unlucky grass has better worth than it.
Delights that had no betters can grow hindmost from their doing:
silver delights that spoil take on ill gifts of old meat
    as no grass does."

You will have been taught that you can't teach an old dog
without breaking eggs—look at one broken egg. But what will
it have taught me? It was an unlucky tide that parted you from
me. You are going off into the night. My night. It was not me
that did the things to you, but a devil—it has always been one
of my tricks never to put off till tomorrow what spoils the
broth. But "poison" is too ill a word for me; "spoiled" and "blind"
may render it, but never could any poison come to you from
me. My words were unlucky. If the winds could have gathered
the other words in my mouth, to be saved and poured from
the sky...! It is that what you have done is a hell for me, a red
burning cloud that has left me burned, and blind.

46

"The kingdom of the blind is paved with good intentions:
In the kingdom of the blind, words will never harm me;
In the kingdom of the blind, God disposes."
   —You can lead a horse to water, but the one-eyed man is king.

In the kingdom of the blind, few are chosen.
In the kingdom of the blind, sailors take warning:
In the kingdom of the blind, unlucky in love.
   Many are called, but the one-eyed man is king.

In the kingdom of the blind, leave no stone unturned.
In the kingdom of the blind, bury their dead.
The kingdom of the blind is another man's poison.
   On the road to Hell, the one-eyed man is king.

Blind days are breaking on sailors in hindmost ports. Waiting to go with the tide. You have me in your hand: before you leave on the tide, dispose of the bones you have gathered. But let me once come and look at you: a sailor's dog, when the sailor goes off, looks on him as leaving for always. Let me come and look at you once before you go, that's all. It's little for you to do. Not that it will be all delight to me—better any time to put off the day of leaving and of leave-taking; but it will be a thing to wait with. A loaf is no gift to a king, but it's a mighty one to a man without meat.

A thing to wait with: for dead days and blind nights. For bread and broth—that's something. Grass will go on growing. Things to do: call the dogs; save time; play cards; lie in the grass; wait for you; go down the road. To look at bushes growing at the roadside—bushes that you grew? The road is broken, water gathers in the stones and grass is growing up. One could call the birds in the bushes to drink the water on the stones and look for worms in the stitches of grass. A cat is playing with one unlucky bird's eggs. Another cat lies dead in the road—no, not dead, sleeping; no, not even sleeping: playing with a mouse. The cat soon takes it up. The unlucky mouse in the cat's mouth is not dead.

VII

The Road

The road to Hell gets the worm.
The road to Hell gathers no moss.
The road to Hell leaves no stone unturned.

The road to Hell from little acorns grows.
The road to Hell is paved with rolling stones.
The road to Hell waits for no man.

The road to Hell takes the hindmost.
The road to Hell has its day.
The road to Hell spoils the broth.

The road to Hell has a silver lining:
The road to Hell wasn't built in a day.
On the road to Hell, do as the Romans do.

VIII

Rolling clouds gathered in the west, and the wind has been blowing from the west, growing from early morning till night. The clouds came early, little at first, a few silver birds that grew into dogs and horses and parted to be new things, mighty things spoiling for a storm. And all day the growing wind. Wind today, wind tomorrow, and a storm coming. Before night storms the sky looks silver-green. The tide too is coming from the west, with the wind. The night rolls in from the east, and from the west the clouds roll up to meet it. Night is the time when winds gather, and all the other winds are pouring down water and grass. Let the winds blow, let the tide build. Let it rain. It *is* raining; and blowing; and the tide will soon be pouring onto stones and grass. Water will gather in tide and sky and with it the wind will pave the kingdom of night. The wind will bury the road to the port with the rendered waters.

As for me, it's time to be sleeping. All the devils of the storm cannot spoil my intention of sleeping early.

Night rolled in from the east, clouds from the west rolled up to it—: what were the words of Mark Twain, East is east and west is west and never the two shall meet? Have met! in the wind. In my kingdom the wind is called—no: when it blows at night in the oaks, the wind is called "kingdom"; in the day, "road." Not "my" kingdom with me king—king's another

man. Sleeping too? Sleeping kings are dead kings. But when a king sleeps, what delights! Stones of time and storm are parted, a new morning sky breaks into the night, and the king's intentions, a little at a time, are built up of silver water, birds, and early clouds. But no king can sleep all night. Kings have been taught that kingdoms are made with poison, it must not be him that is given poison: even when, as kings always must, the king drinks with other men. Kings have been taught that a kingdom is built with broken bones, it mustn't be him that's broken: better that the bones of all the kingdom pave the king's road. Sleeping is soon done for. (And you—don't take poison, not today!) The king gets up, goes to look at the night sky, and the mighty clouds give him delight—an other, one-eyed delight.

Night is the time for giving poison to kings, and for man's love. . . . What are the bushes burning on the road? Take no poison—not today!

Soon not sleeping. Wind and burning. When the wind has mighty intentions, call in your horses and dogs. (But love that looks shy is as an oak in the storm. And no wind can break the oaks, not today, not tomorrow.)

Getting up:

Water is pouring from the night sky. What a wind! It's raining from side to side. The wind has buried the road to the port in sky- and tide-water. The waters meet from time to time and no road is left.

The port sky burns in the night. The storm must be rolling its waters through the port, burying it too. A mighty tide could soon break up the stones of the port. Clouds of water breaking on green stones. . . . When a storm is blowing, let the old sailor in.

Twice the waters have met and rolled down the road. "Dere's a mighty water comin' down de road!" It never rains without breaking eggs, and things play the fool in a storm— water, stones, all the devils and everything but mice and worms! Better to sleep like them. (Do worms sleep?) Better sleep if one can; and one can.

It could be it's raining worms. (Better worms than poison!) Skies *can* rain worms, blown from other grasses. And stones—"a day when stones rained from the sky," the silver sky came down: stones are raining down, the dead lie on every road. Dead every which-what. Red dogs drink green water that breaks from the stones.

> Leave no stone
>   Before you leap,
> Six of one
>   The twain shall meet

The old dead lie in their silver linings, but the new dead lie in stones and water. You chose the dead; you chose the devils. The water takes old bones from the grass and moss, and silver bones roll in a new tide of stones and water. In my kingdom the dead are not buried, the dead are not burned as in other kingdoms, but are left to spoil in the bushes. In my kingdom the dead are not lucky, are not unlucky. In my kingdom the dead wait without gathering time. In my kingdom the dead have no good intentions and no ill ones, cannot give love, cannot take it; but can spoil and save.

Let the dead
  Break my bones,
Better than no bread
  Sticks and stones

Old moss lies on unturned bones. You chose the dead and the devils. The dead are not buried in the blind kingdom of worms and water. It is raining, it has rained today all day and all night. It will rain tomorrow and every day. It has always rained. Days of water—the water will drink up the stones. Will it drink the dead? And what of the king? The king isn't dead. (You chose the dead, you chose the devils!) The king is broken and must be given six stitches. The dead can make fools of kings, but to what good? The king will go on sleeping with six stitches and the water and stones. And soon the king will give up sleeping.

The dead of the West are called "God" and "Caesar."

(Have given up sleeping.)

Cats will have been left dead in the road. In the old days one never left dead cats.

When it blows at night, the wind in the oaks is called "kingdom;" in the day, "road."

IX

Morning, from the east, a mighty sky—an even lining of burning silver clouds, which the new day soon parts.

The storm has spoiled the new grass. It has broken the fences old and new. The kingdom of shy horses lies green and silver in the morning.

The worms have not let the storm spoil their day. Look at their comings and goings! What are they gathering? What's bread for a worm?

And as for my bread—no bread for me today. What to do? Anything, that's what. The road to Hell is better than no bread.

But the break of day proposes new intentions. Look: a loaf of bread has been left for me, by you—you!—and a few words: "...Storm played tricks...Words coming from him that were ill words to me...Fools...No road to Rome, not with him!"

Delight breaks from me as birds break from morning clouds. The unlucky time is done for. Blind days burn away. Time and tide will bury their dead.

When did you come and leave the things, the words and the bread? The gift of the loaf you made was worth many words of love. When did you come in, with me not sleeping? On what night tide, from what other side of the sky—

The clouds have parted and lie before the wind.

That dog in the bushes—dead? sleeping?

What good bread you make! And you have not left me. Love disposes of cats and kings, but a good stitch never parts. Can any man be as lucky? That unturned card was a one-eyed king.

And at night you will come and take me to you. You will not have come too soon. The dead were waiting for me, might have come soon, waiting, paving the road that leads into their kingdom with the green mosses of unlucky delight (delight of sleeping, of going blind, of being one with the night). When you are with me, their poison will be poured away.

Mallarmé Saved, a lucky Caesar, from me as one to bury me, the
      delight-giving,
little-burning stick from a cloud of kings, the red of bones
      as blown water, a thing better than silver, storm!
and to break with delight at the night-red lining proposing,
      on the other side, the intention
of being disposed on the burying stone of me away, as
      for a king?

What! of all that mighty cloud, not as little as one spoiled
      lining
is left, it is the dead of night, in the gathered cloud that
      proposes good things for you and me, with
no other, but for the mighty playing Silver Egg, one
      that looks and calls,
that pours the rolling-cat delight of it, in night with
      no day—

it is of you when the delight were always! from you
always and not other what of God's sky blown away saves
a little king-storm (as of man when little), rained on you
as day breaking, when down on the lying-linings you
      dispose it
as it were the silver trick that an old king's horseman might
      have looked from, given to a shy Caesar and not a man,
      and little;
and from it—to render you—red delights of the bush would
      pour.

62

The new fence was broken in the storm. How the wind must have blown to break it—to blow it down. The fence lay on one side all day. Horses gathered on one side and on the other; the horses came up to the fence and looked at it and at the other horses; but none went onto the others' grass. Today men will come and put the oak fence up and make it as good as new.

The wind is gone, the mighty wind (one to make Caesar wait for a day): today the wind is even, an early wind to be drunk in.

Soon going down: to be met with another gift from you— a dozen red eggs. Gifts should be given with the intention of delight: a gift of new eggs always gives delight (and red eggs are even better). Better than all is the gift of gifts, you, none other, coming to me down road and grass.

You had come to me at night, you came to me in the early morning; and all the day went on in delight. A few words once and for all of him, of you and him, of you and me and him:

"When you were going with him…"

"Don't! It's done with."

"It's done with—but isn't anything left of the love you had for him?"

"It wasn't love—the intention of love, that's all. My one love is for you, it will never be for another. With him it never could have been."

"You waited for love to come, it never comes, it has to be made—take it from me. Have a little bread?"

"All the days gone for nothing—spoiled."

"Rome wasn't built without breaking eggs."

"But for *him*! It wasn't worth it."

"What did the storm do to him—not a man of mighty waters?"

"No—but one of *many* waters: always going off....What made me a sucker for him? A sucker!"

"Never should've let you go off with him—'Never let a sucker even break eggs,' as the teaching goes."

"The storm made me lucky. It taught me what to look for in him: money, and that's all."

"'A fool and his money, sailors take warning'—"

"But 'A stitch in time, sailor's delight'!"

"You can play the card with me today—today, and any day!"

That was that.

Morning is not done when you propose to teach me the love of mice. Love of cat, dog, and horse, good—but love of mouse?

"The shy mouse that never looks at the sky...Wait."

You leave a road of bread for the mice—many roads: a Rome of sticks and moss. The sticks are disposed to make fences at the side of the roads, which are paved with the moss, with the bread broken on it. Soon mice come from grasses and stones, one at a time, and go down the roads gathering the bread: little silver kings.

Red sky at night, the mice will play:
> *"When the cat's away, sleeping dogs lie.*
> *When the cat's away, take it with you.*
> *When the cat's away, what you can do today!"*

In the kingdom of the blind, the mice will play.
  When the cat's away, gather no mouse.
  When the cat's away, the devil take the hind mouse.
  When the cat's away, the one-eyed mouse is king.

When you have taught me mouse love, you propose worms. Worms! Mice and worms may meet in the grass; and mice and worms may never have to drink; but to me a mouse is to a worm as day is to night. You teach me, "The intentions of worms are few but mighty. The night kingdom of worms can break all things. Mighty stones lie on worms and do not harm them. When one is harmed, a worm has a trick of breaking into six or nine and growing into new worms. Today's worm is tomorrow's dozen...."

Worm love is left to another day.

When bread and meat were done with, you took me into the kingdom of clouds and birds: down a new road. Even a fool would have taken delight in being on it, never away from the water, and all green on the other side—oaks and bushes breaking with green. Few grasses have had time to grow on the road, but in the stones acorns are disposing green suckers. You lead me into the oaks and bushes, on old sticks green with moss, on off-red mosses lying on stones from which silver water breaks. You teach me that oaks can have moss on all sides. You teach me to look for bird's eggs, and to part the eggs from the birds without harming one and the other. (Six eggs lay burning-red on moss.) You led me on till, parting the grasses, you looked onto the water that lies to the east. No one had taught me that one could get to it on the new road.

Little clouds wait in the sky; other clouds lie even with the water: no wind. A stick from my hand takes time going away in the water. You let one hand lie in the water—should one go in? You have other intentions.

You lead me down the road to look at horses that can be got for little money—no "My kingdom for a horse" for you! On the grass rolling away from the road, many horses are calling to one another.

Choosing a horse is new to me. What has been taught to me of horses? That a horse has one good side; that when you call a dog it comes, when you call a cat it *may* come, but a horse comes to you without calling.

A red horse takes one of the fences twice. A little horse is coming up to the road—it's taking the road fence! Don't let it get away! A man is coming to get him, stick in hand. (That wouldn't do me any good: taking a stick to a horse would spoil my day.)

It is you that chooses the horse, and what a horse! You propose a little money, wait for a time, and take me away. Tomorrow you will come and you'll get the horse.

You can lead a horse to water without breaking eggs.
  You can lead a horse to water, but do as the Romans do.
  A gift horse is always on the other side of the fence.

You can lead a horse to water and never the twain shall meet.
  You can lead a horse to water, but God disposes.
  Mighty gift horses from little silver linings grow. . . .

Night like day breaks from the east with a silver egg. Many other days are to come. What will new days and nights propose to you and me? The delight of sleeping in the morning— of sleeping all day, lying down in the morning and getting up at night. You will teach me to play cards, you will teach me to grow old. You can take me egg-rolling. You can take me down to the water with a dozen worms. You can teach me, "Save a sailor!" You will teach me every night to look to the morning. You will give me a hand. Saving a little money would be a good thing. You will make things new, and choose green linings to go with the grass and red ones not to. You will take me as God made me. You will lie down with me. You will let time do its tricks. And, from one day to another, one-eyed delight will go on playing with old silver birds.

XI

A storm one day made the meat spoil (not the mighty storm, another one, when many days had come and gone). The meat had spoiled: you had been unlucky in not putting it away with a west wind blowing. With a west wind, worms in meat grow better, and it soon goes all silver and green. And even to you, meat worms are no delight—maybe you once had worms? No, you're a cook, and worms can never be a delight to a cook. That is what is good with omelets: never a worm.

The wind had spoiled the meat, and with it your delight in making meat, broth, bread, omelets, and other things. Once you had a cook. ("What did he leave for?" "Too many cooks are soon parted.") The day had come, you gathered, to have another.

At the time, the cooks of many kingdoms had chosen the

port down the road for a mighty gathering; and you took me with you to choose a new cook from the ones that had come.

The port was as it had been before—the storm had broken it up, but it had been built new. Not many sailors had been taken by the storm. The tide can play tricks with sailors, as can the wind, but on the day of the storm, wind and tide led many sailors into port in time.

What tide and wind are to sailors, meat and broth are to cooks: and in the port the words "meat" and "broth" were in every mouth (and "egg" too).

(Were any of the cooks sailors, any of the sailors cooks? To be at once a cook and sailor is to be twice king.)

Choosing a cook is a mighty thing. Time can make even fools into good cooks, but it is better to have a good one from the word go. You must have money—money can make and break kings, and it may even get one a cook; but a good cook? A good cook can dispose of kings. You must get the cook's love too, with one thing and another. The love of a *good* cook is better than any king's—it is worth the kingdom of God.

But for cooks good and ill, money is good to have. "Too many cooks have a silver lining" are the words in which you rendered it. But you went on (when many cooks had not taken up what you were proposing), "'Too many cooks' *has* a silver lining, too: six of one would be better than no bread!" Too many cooks, but few are chosen—or choose. It was night before one was disposed to come away with you.

"When the omelet's away,
The eggs will play"
—FRENCH
PROVERB

You can't make an omelet with good intentions:
Too many cooks are better than no bread.
One man's meat, as good as a mile,
Once burned, spoils the broth.
Too many cooks are worth two in the bush-
You can't make an omelet on the other side of the fence.
Half a loaf is better than two in the bush-
Half a loaf in a storm!
It's an ill wind that spoils the broth.

You can't make an omelet—but few are chosen:
A fool and his money are better than no bread.
One man's meat gets the worm—
Look before you spoil the broth!
Too many cooks take the hindmost.
(One man's meat is greener on the other side of the fence....
Half a loaf is better than no silver lining.
Half a loaf is better without breaking eggs:
Man proposes, and spoils the broth.

You can't make an omelet, and God disposes.
One man's meat is better than no bread.
One man's meat is worth two in the bush.
(Sticks and stones spoil the broth.)
Too many cooks, twice shy.
Half a loaf is better than the other side of the fence.
Half a loaf is as good as a mile.
Half a loaf has its day.
Many are called, but spoil the broth.

Many days came and went, good ones; till today, when the cook let the meat burn. The cook was sleeping, and unturned meat soon burns. Sleeping—in the daytime? You do not have to be taught that cooks drink: a cook may always have to have water at hand, but it isn't for drinking. Sleeping in the daytime, and sleeping all night too, with the birds and the other cooks. You had been ill-disposed to him before, and your words to him were unlucky ones—calling him a fool and proposing that good cooks were dead cooks. The cook went all red and soon was gone; and all the money you had given him was gone with the wind...with the cook....Too many cooks wait for no man.

The meat has burned—and red meat is good for the drinking man; but save the bones for the broth and the broth for tomorrow's meat. Bones make for good broth, and good broth makes a mighty man. Put in any old meat you have, too—it can render good broth.

You give me the broth and make an omelet. You teach me that it should be made without water, and that when making it a good thing is to roll it. It's time for bread and eggs. Save a little bread to gather up what will be left of the omelet.

You have made better omelets before.

Dead cooks do not make better cooks—that is what the day has taught me.

XII

Once burned,
Leave no stone unturned.
Twice shy,
Let sleeping dogs lie.

Days have come and will come, todays and tomorrows, todays paved with tomorrows and with days that are gone. The tomorrows lie on today as the dead do. It is time to give them up.

As cats gather mice, as ports gather sailors, you gather old intentions. Every day you gather me and put me away. You have called me a king, but you look on me as the bones of today that will soon be dead, you put the day away with me, the "king." Don't take the king for the kingdom. The kingdom is today.

Tomorrow can be intention, but today does not wait: it is delight or not. The morning is the one morning, or no morning. Delight as to the grass-gathering horse. The dog's mouth cannot put off the time when it will take up the bone. Cards are given to me, to you. Every card takes a trick, and one lucky card is worth a kingdom.

Today breaks into little winds, roads, clouds. The wind that comes from the tide of clouds is gathering intentions, of silver days and of storms. Don't wait for it. The time that will come "soon" has come today. All roads "take it with you." Tomorrow is for the birds—the early birds that look away to tomorrow. But the early bird must come down.

Oaks are growing and gathering their linings of green. Moss gathers on oaks, on sticks of dead oak, on stones. Grass grows and soon is dead, and grows new, and the dead grass is taken into the kingdoms of birds, mice, and worms. In the morning, sticks are being gathered and broken. It's time to go into the day. Sticks are gathered at the water side, and dead oak that makes for good burning burns. Dead grass too burns at the road side.

It is time to go blind into the day. Let the blind dog that you led lead you. Dead times grow in the grass, in the oaks (the dead are parted from none), but from them oaks and grass

grow new. Time to give up one thing and another (but take one gift from me). Let everything go. Let everyone go—let the cook be gone! The time has come to let it all go. Give what you can. Put silver money in the blind man's hands. (But money is a little gift, and gathers little men. "For a cook a gift of silver, for a sailor a gift of time, for a good man a gift of love.") Give bones to the old dog, give broth and meat to the old man lying at the side of the road. Spoil the mighty horse that has broken down. But for you, take the day that is today; and the night with it.

Red bones break in the old dog's mouth.

It will be night all too soon. In the west, birds will part the lining of day. The day will break down, and clouds burn for it.

It will soon be night, and soon tomorrow. The cards will lie unturned. The horses, having drunk, will sleep. Mice will take to their little roads. The sleeping logs die. The birds are disposed in the oaks for the night. And the worms—what do worms do in the night, blind things? Do worms gather when parting meat from bone?

Night comes, time to make broth and meat. You cannot let everyone in. But let the dog in, and the cat, and me. The kingdoms will soon be sleeping, for tomorrow. And for tomorrow—for tomorrow bury the dead things of today. Bury and burn the always-old things; pour off the rest:

Burn a dozen and one cards. Bury a few acorns. Pour off the even tide. Bury the poison-birds and the cook's lucky dog and cat. Burn the grass devils and half the night. Pour off the ill waters. Burn the sides and linings of things, the cloud men, and the better Other. Pour off the rolling wind. Bury the little tricks, the unlucky sailor, the stone mouth, and the mice dead from poison. Bury the loaf storms. Burn the bone fences. Burn the oak sticks and another day. Bury the old horse and the unturned moss. Pour off the eggs. Bury the sleeping hands,

the green breaks, and the hindmost road. Burn delights and intentions (the twain) and their time-bushes. Pour off the fool's words and the others. Burn the nine gods and every gift, the good stitches and the new suckers. Bury Rome and Caesar, the kingdom and the king, and the hell in the red west. Pour off the early morning. Burn the new port, the oak sticks, and the one-eyed sky. Bury any love. Burn the silver east. Bury meats and omelets, and pour off the mighty broth.

The burning fences make red stitches in the lining of the sky.

Red clouds dispose the night.

FIRST DERIVATIONS

PERVERBS AND PARAPHRASES

"The sky was clear except for the fog rising to the east—fermentation from the oak bog" is a *paraphrase* of the *perverb* "Every cloud from little acorns grows."

Paraphrases I

1

...slithering its irresistible way under paving-stone and cobblestone, under laterite and asphalt, under packed earth and concrete, from the first footpath to the last speedway...

2

"Not only land—a village!"
"They'll intern us, you know."
"They'll feed us, too."

3

"Cazzo!" shrieked the myna bird on her wrist. We got a baleful look from the waiter, among others; I felt the cars in the Piazza del Popolo had slowed down at the word.

Alexandra sighed, "He used to say 'shithead'."

4

If they left at dawn, they could that day drive the slow-moving herd a *koqlak* farther [about 1750 yards]; if they waited for their uncle, he would supply them with enough dried goose to save them, in hunting, the time lost by delaying their departure. They argued their dilemma into the night.

5

"…and I would prefer, in place of 'not live by it alone,' 'not live by it at all.' If I had to choose between renouncing the things I love, and starving, I would rather starve. And what are the things I love, these ever-so-precious things? Why, the glories of sunup and sundown; the hounds that slumber at my feet every night (and not only them, good fortunate creatures that they are, but also the meanest stray I may encounter); the sparrow that flies up to eat between my fingers; the passage of the seasons year after year; and day after day, the ebb and flow of the eternal seas."

6

I edged my hand along the gunnel, seized the noddy by its legs, and snapped its neck. For the first time since our craft had foundered, Michael's bearded, peeling face broke into a smile.

7

The cawing of the crow as it flew past his window irritated Webster. It was just dawn, and he liked to sleep late Sundays. Then he thought, why should a crow be flying this way so early? Listening, he heard a fainter sound—axe against wood. He got up and saw from his window that on the far side of his field a man was chopping down a Lombardy poplar, one of a row of eleven that Webster had planted fifteen years before. The trees now topped the neighboring beeches.

The man with the axe must be Friedlander. He'd complained about the trees, claiming their shade spoiled the pasture grass beyond them. He was trying to take advantage of Webster's Sunday sleep to get rid of them.

Webster put on pants and shoes and took down his shotgun. Going out of the door, he saw that Friedlander had felled one tree and had set to work on a second, and he started to run across the wide, wet field.

8

See No. 4.

9

Cold chicken for breakfast is not my custom, but I was damned if I'd fight on an empty stomach.

10

See No. 7.

11

What was it that made things go wrong? The rooster that woke me up at dawn so that I was tired and careless? Being concerned about Tim and Tina, snoring away on the kitchen floor when they should have been running around? That rock Johnny bowled across the lawn onto the cellar-door? It gave me such a start! The weather was getting stormy (should have known what was coming from that rosy-fingered dawn!), and things do turn whenever that happens. Charles said it was the fault of ghosts, no point trying to stop them—of course he *would* say that: he's the one who claimed a single spoonful of cream wasn't enough, there ought to be half a dozen at least. Then Johnny snitched my bread for his snack—didn't leave any more than he took, the rascal! Whatever, I'm not serving this soup to anyone.

Maybe *all* these things were responsible. But my bet is it was the poodles. You can't cook properly with them around. Not because they're poodles, naturally. They happen to be a race I adore.

The Chinese speaker harangued them on the advantages of socialism, the American on those of capitalism. Barracked within the barbed-wire confines of the settlement, they thought only of the lost hills of Hebron and Khalasah.

They use the yolks not only for diagnosis but to find out directions on sunless days. My pocket compass was a revelation to them.

14

She imagined that for the rain to pour down on her so, all the vapors in heaven must be concentrated above her head; that to make such a din, the hounds yelping behind her must have gathered from the four corners of the earth. Then the boulder against which she was leaning sagged away from her, tumbling into the gorge. Her endurance spent, she sank weeping to the muddy ground.

15

"On the 21st, we'll study cirrocumulus stratiformis; on the 22nd, cirrocumulus castellanus; on the 23rd, cirrocumulus floccus. That is, if it doesn't rain."

16

See No. 11.

17

Billowing and seeping, the bitter gas punished those least deserving it—local inhabitants trapped in their apartments, old men and women, bystanders who didn't know there was anything to run from.

18

See No. 14.

See No. 5.

See No. 11.

He should have taken the whole bread with him and not split it in two. The hard crust of what he had left was intact, the crumb hopelessly maggot-ridden.

Long before coming for the Pope's sanction, St. Francis made a pilgrimage here, prompted by remorse at refusing a leper's offer to share his bread with him.

See No. 11

He had eaten forty uncooked carobs. He didn't regret it, since they were his first food in several days; but it was the first time in his life he had to walk away from his own farts.

The cave was an adequate refuge, and provided welcome coolness by day. After dark it became a nightmare: dozens, perhaps hundreds of bats swarmed into it, pressing towards the back along the passage where I lay, which was so small that the creatures could not help scraping along my prone body. Within seconds their claws covered my skin with tiny cuts. I crawled out quickly, even though I knew the sentries were passing within a hundred feet of me.

At dawn I returned to the cave. A new torment awaited me: mosquitoes, of which I had noticed only a few the day before, attacked me in myriads, drawn to my wounds like filings to a magnet. Only the terror of capture and of the certain torture it would bring kept me hidden. I prayed for night to come.

As soon as darkness fell, I emerged once again. For several hours the bats had the cave to themselves. They left me alone, of course. During this time I dared a foray to the spring below and filled my nearly empty canteen.

There was no respite from the mosquitoes the following morning. In anticipation of them I swathed every exposed inch of skin in clothing. It was then, as I lay in sweating misery, that it occurred to me that these pests might be the very thing that attracted the bats to the place.

There was a stagnant pool, more mudhole than pool, at the back of the cave; it was formed by a minute trickle that filtered from the rock ceiling. It might well be the breeding-place of the insects, whose presence in this desert region was certainly anomalous.

The exiguity of my hole made it impossible to turn around in it and so act at once. That evening, before starting my out-of-

doors vigil, I re-entered the cave headfirst; and removing from my knapsack a can of lubricating oil, I emptied most of it onto the shallow puddle. If all went well, the oil would spread over the surface and suffocate the larvae in the water. The bats would eliminate those already hatched.

I was right. Next morning my daytime tormentors were markedly fewer. I was even able to uncover my head from time to time. At night, when I had left the cave, the bats returned in fewer numbers and for a shorter time: their food supply was disappearing. Indeed, that night they must have destroyed it entirely, for during the days that followed I was not bitten once.

Thanks to my meagre but adequate provisions and the water from the spring, I held out until the soldiers decamped. During the remaining nights, aside from an occasional solitary, the bats abandoned my cave altogether. I almost missed them.

26

You keep telling me the drought will last all year. And I tell you I don't give a damn what you say.

27

Milos showed us the grove of ilex from which the sacred trumpets are made. Only young trees were used, since the wood of the larger ones produces a gruff tone.

Perverbs I (in random order)

It never rains, but words will never harm me
Every cloud spoils the broth
The early bird saves nine
Every dog in a storm
The early bird has a silver lining
All roads get the worm
Half a loaf spoils the broth
Every cloud takes the hindmost
The early bird is as good as a mile
It's a mighty oak that blows no good
An ill wind is better than no bread
The early bird is better than no bread
Every cloud in a storm
In the kingdom of the blind, spoil the broth
Bird in the hand, sailor's delight
East is east and west is west on the other side of the fence
Every cloud has its day
A bird in the hand does as the Romans do
Every dog is better than no bread
A bird in the hand is better than no bread
The early bird spoils the broth
Any port is better than no bread
East is east and west is west without breaking eggs
A bird in the hand is as good as a mile
Half a loaf leads to Rome
Every dog spoils the broth
Half a loaf gets the worm

Sorites for a Rich Indian Uncle

Premises
  1. Lucky at cards is better than no bread, and half a loaf is soon parted;
  2. Sticks and stones are another man's poison;
  3. A rolling stone leaves no stone unturned and gathers the hindmost;
  4. Lucky at cards, twice shy: let sleeping dogs take the hindmost;
  5. Half a loaf gathers no moss, and a rolling stone gathers no silver linings;
  6. When half a loaf is another man's poison, let half a loaf lie;
  7. Never give sticks and stones an even break;
  8. Once burned, unlucky in love;
  9. When half a loaf spoils the broth, never give half a loaf an even break;
  10. A rolling stone waits for no man (sailors take warning);
  11. When a rolling stone spoils the broth, let sticks and stones lie;
  12. Sticks and stones, unlucky in love—but look before you take the hindmost;
  13. When a rolling stone has its day, sticks and stones are soon parted;
  14. Half a loaf, unlucky in love—and a rolling stone, unlucky in love;
  15. A rolling stone gathers no good intentions;
  16. You can't teach sticks and stones new tricks;
  17. Lucky at cards and God disposes, but sticks and stones wait for no man.

Conclusion
  Never give a rolling stone an even break.

28

The hatch opened. The slipstream was roaring like a hundred angry beasts, each warning me to step back. I hooked up my chute-ring and jumped.

29

In ordinary circumstances his verboseness was less than dangerous. But compounded by a generous desire to share with his audience every detail of his money-making scheme, it produced a lecture so interminable that captain and officers fell asleep and failed to notice the clear portents of the ship's impending doom.

30

Known for its power to bring on severe headache and nervous collapse, the sirocco this year claimed a man's life. The coroner reported death by asphyxiation, citing the oppressive weather. The deceased was unknown on this island.

31

See No. 11.

"You always win!" he shouted across the table, on which his kings and my aces lay upturned. His remark, although violent in tone, implied no physical threat, and I ignored it.

33

He had won forty thousand francs at trente et quarante, forty thousand dollars at chemmy, and after the casino closed, forty thousand pounds in a private poker game. Yet when I suggested he celebrate and have some champagne, he did not even answer but raised his eyes to heaven and cut the deck.

34

Her failure to win the nomination was not her fault but her sponsor's. When he arrived at the convention, he was the unwitting host of a *Taenia solium* that had just begun budding off reproductive segments, or proglottides, into his intestine. As he mounted the rostrum, the irresistible slipping through his anus of the first proglottis filled him with deep alarm, and subsequent ones reduced him to a sweating ghost of himself, so that instead of the energetic speech that was to crown a successful campaign, he made a confusing plea that in ten stuttering minutes ruined her chances for good.

35

"Scotch? Vodka? Cold Duck?"
"Whatever you say."
"Never touch the stuff!"

36

I phoned Greenville and Memphis; St. Louis; Des Moines and Sioux City; even Fort Yates. They all had the same story to tell, and I knew the levees would be going soon.

37

We learned that the twin sisters had inherited a huge fortune, and that one condition of the inheritance was that they marry men capable of telling them apart. We were also informed that the two women would receive, separately, any of the citizens of the town who aspired to become the husband of either.

Bachelors, widowers, and divorced men (and some not divorced) presented their candidacies. The men were summoned to the hotel one by one. There, each was first introduced into one sister's apartment, then, having made her acquaintance, into the other's, which was on an adjacent floor. Each paid several calls before trying to guess their identities, but in the end none guessed correctly; nor could he have, since Kathleen and Charlotte were one and the same. Quick-change artistry and a service elevator enabled the one girl to reappear transformed in the second apartment before the candidate had been guided to it by her partners through corridors and stairways. By the time of his failure, the suitor was usually so excited by the fair "sisters'" encouragement of his suit and by the signs of high living that had been craftily displayed to him, that he fell a ready victim to the confidence men into whose hands he had played.

38

Acorns taste bad, and the bark is even worse, especially on trees as old as these. But what can we do?

39

Standing in the ruined church, he followed his memory back to the remote, festive day he had first seen it, as a page at his sister's wedding. He had, he recollected, been dressed in stiff, sprigged white stuffs. He had resented his sister for the role thrust on him. He had been very bored. Barely conscious of the priest's Latin words, he had whiled away the time rolling in his gloved fingers three acorns picked up in the churchyard; he had aimed them at a crack in the dusty mosaic of the floor, finally pressing them into the crevice with the toe of his slipper.

Two stout trees now grew where he once had stood. In their ascent towards the light of the gutted roof they had split open the floor and overturned the altar. The foot-thick slab of onyx on which the chalice had rested now lay in shattered irregular pieces, each still monumental under its springy mantle of periwinkle.

40

"Are acorns bitter?! Don't you remember when we were camping and some fell in the soup?"

41

At Francorchamps a cyclone of great violence interrupted the Belgian Grand Prix after three laps. Drivers were obliged

to abandon their cars when the tornado struck. Nebbiola, who was trailing the field, sought shelter in a forest through which the track runs and was killed when two large trees fell and crushed him. He was identified by a ring on his left hand, which protruded from beneath one trunk, clutching an acorn.

42

"Six weeks I've traveled to reach Dodona, and because I'm one day late you tell me I cannot consult the oracle?"

But the Praetor fumed in vain.

43

When I ran onto the platform and saw that the train was already pulling out, I started to cry. Even if he hadn't given me the job he could have let me have money to tide me over. Then, dabbing my eyes, I looked down and saw the lottery ticket.

44

In his curious English that his difficulty in pronouncing *r*'s made positively quaint, he said that if I insisted on finishing everything that evening I would never reach the station in time for my fiancé's arrival.

45

A funny twist appeared in later generations: they lost the urge to start the game at all. They inherited a knowledge of the rules without any impulse to use them—two traits that

had seemed so completely linked we never dreamed they were separable. We tried all kinds of prodding to get them to perform, and finally settled on a low-power electric grid in the floor of the cage, which gives them a series of shocks when we want to test them. It's never failed so far, and we've reached our thirtieth generation with perfect "Capture the flag" capabilities. The only bad effect is microscopic blisters under the paws.

46

In another version of the Polyphemus myth, the blinding with the lighted stake is part of the ritual enthronement of the Cyclops in his royal functions.

47

"The sun behind the grayness at tempest's end—that," said the Solitary, "is joy and sustenance to me!"

48

Between the opening of his hamburger stand opposite St. Peter's and the day when the Michelin Guide raised his restaurant to the "worth a trip" category (specialty: *bistecca tritata alla Giovanni XXIII*), half a dozen competitors had already capitalized on the new fashion he had started.

49

During a holiday in northern Montana, an amateur trapper was cooking his supper one evening when eight draft resisters invaded his camp. For several days, in the course of which they went without food, they had been looking in vain for the Canadian border. At first they threatened him, but he was delighted to share his bear steaks.

50

See No. 5.

51

With that sunrise, it looks like we're in for a bad day. Weasels out near the house, another sure sign—and look at those little fellas scampering down the stairs! Must've come from the attic.

52

Each noon he noticed (so he thought) her ever more assiduous avoidance of him. Every evening he went to sleep imagining that she would elude him until he died from grief. Pacific suns rose and set in invariable splendor, and still his heart yearned in vain.

53

See No. 52.

54

See No. 5.

Perverbs II (in random order)

Never put off till tomorrow and never the twain shall meet
Mighty oaks are better than no bread
It's an ill wind before you leap
A miss is as good as a silver lining
It's an ill wind that blows with good intentions
Many are called but never the twain shall meet
Lucky at cards, but words will never harm me
Many are called, but it pours
Red sky at morning, unlucky in love
Once burned, the mice will play
Let the dead spoil the broth
Red sky at morning, twice shy
Red sky at night is better than no bread
Mighty oaks leave no stone unturned
Man proposes, but you can't make him drink
One man's meat leads to Rome
Once burned, the one-eyed man is king
Red sky at morning, the mice will play
One man's meat is a silver lining
Mighty oaks wait for no man
Man proposes and gets the worm
Red sky at morning is better than no bread
It's an ill wind that's another man's poison
One man's meat saves nine
Mighty oaks take the hindmost
Mighty oaks spoil the broth
Lucky at cards, but you can't make him drink

Snips of the Tongue

Once burned, twice snide

+

Every drug has its day

+

The road to help is paved with good intentions

+

Never pull off tomorrow what you can do today

+

When in Rome, do as the Trojans do

+

Half a loan is better than no bread

+

Every crowd has a silver lining

+

One man's meat is another man's person

+

Look before you leave

+

A snitch in time saves nine

In the kingdom of the blind, the one-eyed man is kinky

+

Too many cooks spoil the dwarf

55

This variety of rock barnacle not only exhibits an inverse photosensitive reaction to sunlight, but it is capable of anticipating that reaction. If a bright sunset foretells fair weather, for instance, the barnacles start retracting long before dawn so as to avoid exposure to the coming day.

56

See No. 52.

57

See No. 52.

58

See No. 14.

59

For weeks they stored in their coolest cellar all that their hens, ducks and geese laid, then rode with it up to Rome at no more than an amble, careful lest they break any part of the fragile load with which they were to pay their tax.

60

How many centuries the river must have washed those granite chips to make perfect spheres of them! We used one to replace the defective bearing. It held until nightfall, and by then we could see the lights of Alma Ata.

61

The sound of a small avalanche startled me from my torpor. As I watched the rocks bouncing down into the gorge, it occurred to me that in their descent some at least must cross the mushroom-rich cluster of pines. When all was still, I hastened to examine them, and, sure enough, one bore smears of crushed fungus. I licked it greedily.

62

See No. 11.

63

"You say a *nakana* is equal to 879.9 feet?" the surveyor asked. "What a break!"

See No. 48.

Five of us formed a ring, turning endlessly to keep our-
selves warm, and sheltering in the middle of our circle the
person whose turn it was to rest. Thus we survived the bliz-
zard.

66

Thus it was Miranda, imprisoned in that Antwerp attic,
who discovered the remains of the funeral cake baked a cen-
tury before. Its mass had long since crumbled into dust. All
that remained was the chronogram of ten words inscribed on
it:

> "yes I, I'LL DIe for bonnIe CharLIe"
> & so she DIeD

1756, the sum of those letters that could be read as Roman
numerals, was indeed the year of Lucy Reid's death. And now
she, Miranda, was captive in the very same house and threat-
ened with an end as miserable (and wanting furthermore any
redeeming pathos). However, she was not yet dead, and as
long as she breathed she was determined to be mistress of her
fate.

She discovered that the numerical letters were not of the
same substance as the others (those were a kind of papier
maché), and further inspection revealed them to be icing, hard-
ened but unspoiled. That they had not been devoured by ro-
dents during so long a time was yet another testimony to Flem-
ish cleanliness.

Here then was welcome nourishment. To begin her meal, Miranda picked out the *i*'s, nibbling them timorously at first, then eagerly as the hunger brought on by thirty hours' fasting was revived by her sweet bites. Soon, however, the dusty brittleness of the food discouraged her appetite, and it was only through resolution that she absorbed the *c*'s, *d*'s, and *l*'s.

67

She stood in the adjoining field and waved something at us—half a dozen stiff dollar bills. They glowed with extraordinary vividness.

68

Two colossal representations of the Trinity had been raised on the Via Appia Antica, the second immediately outside the city gates.

69

See No. 11.

70

They met in the square at noon. She was, to his relief, alone. "He hasn't come. If he isn't here in an hour, I'll leave with you."

Minutes passed and refused to pass. He could not see how anyone possessed of legs could fail to appear in the time-chasm in which he found himself.

At twelve-thirty he allowed himself a cigarette, another one ten minutes after the first. At twelve forty-five he ordered a drink, which he did not touch (any more than his stifled hopes) until ten minutes before the hour. Four minutes later, as joy seeped deliriously into his limbs, a middle-aged man appeared at the corner of the square, his face shadowed by a broad-brimmed felt hat. At his sight Daisy leapt from her chair and buried herself in his outstretched arms.

71

You've had five warnings already. Your time is up.

72

See No. 5.

73

What started the arduous transformation of belief that brought me at last under the Virgin's mantle? The vision, one winter evening, of the ineffable peace expressed on the faces of my three bassets as they lay in front of the fire, dreaming eternal dreams.

74

See No. 11.

75

As its name indicates, the game requires a few elongated pieces of wood, some rocks, and six objects which can be anything not wood or rock.

76

Sprouting up through the baptistery near the church, other oaks had broken it into a chaos of shattered beams and rocks.

77

"Like 'Ozymandias'!" one observed.

They gazed at the rubble of splintered teak and marble that, not long since, had been reared to the glory of gods and men, and on which, in the midst of a dry plain once rich in woods and grain, not even the least trace of green could be observed.

78

See No. 77.

79

Her father at first swore that he would suffer the fate of Saints Stephen and Andrew rather than let her frequent "that uppity Sam Clemens."

80

"Beat me with staves, pelt me with rocks: in my verses the Muses still shall live!" These were his last words. We have not given up hope of some day finding his poems.

81

Max smashed the truncheon across the bridge of my nose, Tony screwed the slabs sandwiching my right hand a notch tighter. They were approaching the point of permanent damage. I just kept grunting out the truth: I had spent thirteen hours with Phang, but there had been no way to administer the poison—in all that time he had not once raised to his lips as much as a glass of water or a cup of tea.

Perverbs III (in random order)

Six of one wait for no man
Six of one spoil the broth
Six of one, unlucky in love
Six of one are as good as a mile
Render unto Caesar without breaking eggs
Red sky at night, never the twain shall meet
Red sky at night, little acorns
Sleeping dogs are better than no bread
Six of one is better than no bread
A rolling stone spoils the broth
Six of one lead to Rome
A rolling stone in a storm
Six of one do as the Romans do
A rolling stone is better than no bread
Sticks and stones may break my bones, but words save nine
Sleeping dogs lead to Rome
Six of one in a storm
Red sky at night, unlucky in love
A rolling stone has its day
Sticks and stones have their day
Six of one is greener on the other side of the fence
Sticks and stones may break my bones, but you can't make
    him drink
Sleeping dogs spoil the broth
Sticks and stones may break my bones, but never the twain
    shall meet
Sticks and stones and half a dozen of the other
Sticks and stones from little acorns grow
Sticks and stones gather no moss

An Interview with Chairman Mao Tsetung

> "What in the West is a thing, in the
> East is an intention."
>
> —CHINESE PROVERB

Chairman Mao Tsetung, how do you reconcile China's policy of cooperation with the us with the essential hostility of capitalism and communism?

—Look before you wait for no man.

With this attitude in mind, Chairman Mao, your insistence that the process of historical contradiction extends to such advanced groups as the Central Committee of the Party seems surprising. Would you comment on this?

—One Mao's meat is another Mao's poison.

Mr. Chairman, while the Party is severe with recent political enemies, it is apparently willing to forgive those of the prerevolutionary period, for instance Chiang Kai-Shek. Why is this so?

—Let the dead bury their little acorns.

You don't think, Mr. Chairman, that such men could be persuaded to accept or at least understand your views?

—You can't teach every sleeping dog new tricks.

Mr. Mao, why has the Party always insisted on the inculcation, almost by rote, of politically correct thinking on a national scale, even when this has jeopardized economic progress and military preparedness?

—In the kingdom of sticks and stones, the word is king.

On the other hand, Mr. Chairman, you have also insisted on periodic shake-ups of the Party and administration, thus threatening the political unity so painfully acquired.

—You can't make an omelet before you leap.

The time comes when the omelet is made and leaping is out of order. How can one then balance revolution and stability?

—Look before you leave no stone unturned.

What is your response to Chairman Brezhnev's accusation that you have "broken the omelet as well as the eggs"?

—East is east, and West is west, and words will never harm me.

Mr. Chairman, during your long membership in the Party, adversity forced you again and again to postpone your dreams of a better China. How did you find the patience to carry on?

—Time and tide weren't built in a day.

Mr. Chairman, if as some say the pace of revolution here is slackening, aren't you afraid that a decline in new achievements will imperil what has been accomplished already?

—"Without breaking eggs
    In the kingdom of the blind
   New tricks
    Save nine."

I see. But, Chairman Mao Tsetung, as your life approaches its end, don't you feel like hurrying things up and finishing the great work while you are around to see it?

—Time and tide wait for Mao.

82

The San Francisco Giants were near victims of the earthquake. As their bus approached Los Angeles, where they were scheduled to play, it was tipped off the freeway into a deep ravine. But a landslide had already cluttered the gulch with a debris of rock and wood, and the bus came to rest after a drop of only two feet.

83

After Gregory XIII's reform of the leap-year intercalation, there briefly appeared on the Roll of Saints a St. Calendaria, whose feast was celebrated every four years. Was she, or her name, a relic of Juno Kalendaris? Her career was too short for us ever to know.

84

Putting down his sailmaker's needle, the hangman bit off the ends of cord dangling from the mended slip-knot. The noose was now fit for use, and none too soon: dawn was breaking.

85

"You'd better change your habits then, or you'll get nothing to eat at all."

86

When the bosun ordered the sail patched at once, the hands should have sensed that concern for so small a rent augured foul weather.

87

(a) "Madam," the guest advised, "unless you quickly mend the toe of that stocking, your Christmas charity is going to end up in the coal scuttle."

(b) The prime minister had made a public vow, if the negotiations had not succeeded by midnight of that day, to leave the conference and resume the war. Midnight came and went and it was not until a few hours later that agreement was reached. The prime minister wisely disregarded the delay, declared his conditions met, and peace, for France, was secured.

88

See No. 5.

89

There was no point arguing. I told Jim and Jane to do it their way; two days later they set out for Konjo overland. At the time the Muyu was navigable for no more than five miles inland, even in a canoe. So I waited. In three weeks the rains started. Two weeks after that it was possible, at those hours of the day when the ocean added its flood to the river waters, to pass the mile-long sandbar that had been so formidable an obstacle. In my outboard I made it to Konjo in five days' easy

running, and when Jim and Jane arrived two hours later, I was waiting for them with a small feast of pig and beer.

90

His amiability in lending the justices the presidential yacht nearly led to disaster: with the entire Supreme Court aboard for its annual picnic, the ship was caught in a violent summer storm and run against a sandbar. There, already foundering, it risked being broken up by the surf and wind. By good luck, in that very hour ebb changed to flood, and before further harm was done, the rising ocean lifted the boat and its august cargo into the milder waters of Chesapeake Bay.

91

Was I in Paris in May '68? Was I ever! It was the greatest time of my life. I'll never forget one evening at the Tour d'Argent: only six customers, and umpteen chefs knocking themselves out for us.

92

Before they went ashore, he warned his men about Burger Beach, the quarter, "famous" for its food, that stretched along more than five thousand feet of waterfront. They were sure to find indifferent fare at high prices: the local chefs were recruited from other parts of the country among the cast-offs of better restaurants.

"There are four dozen shells in the garbage can—four dozen for three omelets?"

"Madame, eet eez a professional 'azard."

"It appears that on more than one occasion a customer who died after eating here was surreptitiously laid to rest in the garden behind the kitchen. Monsieur Triquet is by no means the first restaurateur, *hélas,* to follow such practices."

"He started here washing dishes. Before that his only experience seems to have been feeding mast to his father's truffle-hogs; and he's not the only one to have started that way, not by a long shot. There must be a chef's mafia recruiting down there."

See No. 92.

See No. 92.

She had ordered each specialty brought to their table by the man who had prepared it, thinking that he would be de-

lighted, flattered—but when the *pâtissier* presented his salver of iced meringues, he left in disgust. She never saw him again.

99

It turned out that installing air vents in the floor added little to the comfort of the staff and precipitated a rise in the incidence of athlete's foot, housemaid's knee, menstrual cramp, and fulminating colitis.

100

Centuries of tide had shifted the wreck into a horizontal breach in the submarine cliff face; and raising it seemed impossible until one of the engineers realized that the cleft had formed between two strata, the upper of limestone, the lower of pumice. He convinced the salvage team that it would be possible by drilling to cut away a floating stone platform under the hulk on which it could be pulled free of the overhang. This was done; and the pumice not only supported the ship during its lateral displacement but proved buoyant enough to raise it unaided, even if with imperceptible slowness, to the ocean surface. It was the rare white pumice described by Cousteau and the elder Pliny—a fact alluded to in the log of the operation: "Most certainly to be marked with a white stone."

101

I clapped my hands and cheered. But not the old balloon-maker. Watching the clumsy biplane lumber off the ground left him sick with despair.

The grapefruit-size balls of thin, crisp, perfectly smooth pastry had been baked around a core of helium, so that now, as the cloches were lifted from the platters, they floated into the air. The kohl-eyed ladies laughingly batted them back and forth. Squatting by the wall, Hassan prayed for one to drift his way. He had eaten nothing for three days.

(a) It seems incredible that I could forget so attractive a proposition for an hour, to say nothing of several days. Ten thousand dollars for two weeks' work on a subject that fascinated me—the Flying Walendas. Perhaps it just seemed too good to be true. Luckily, before the week was over, I went to a matinee of Pasolini's *Teorema,* where the sight of Laura Betti suspended over the Parmesan landscape brought me to my senses. I left the theatre at once, went home and packed, and arrived on schedule next day at Cinecittà.

(b) She had expected her long ascent to bring her face to face with the heavenly host singing hymns of transcendental joy. Instead, she found herself in an obscure gallery of the Vatican museums, confronted with a slovenly guard who followed her whichever way she went, delivering an interminable encomium on fourth century brass coins.

The starter at Chase Manhattan Plaza was adamant.

"My orders are to get one elevator moving every thirty seconds, no matter who's coming through the door—even you, Mr. Rockefeller."

105

We were overcome with joy when we learned that our captain had abolished flogging.

106

"You do it time after time. I keep telling you to let it sit longer in the pan, you never listen, and here we are again with egg-run on the tablecloth."

Perverbs IV (in random order)

A stitch in time saves good intentions
Too many cooks bury their dead
Too many cooks from little acorns grow
What goes up leads to Rome
A stitch in time is another man's poison
What goes up waits for no man
Time and tide are better than no bread
Too many cooks must come down
Too many cooks and half a dozen of the other
When the cat's away, sailors' delight
What goes up has its day
What goes up is better than no bread
Time and tide are worth two in the bush
Too many cooks break eggs
You can't make an omelet but it pours
A stitch in time is better than no bread
What goes up blows no good
Time and tide saves nine
A stitch in time, sailors take warning
What goes up is another man's poison
A stitch in time has its day
Too many cooks, sailors take warning
Sticks and stones save nine
Too many cooks are as good as a mile
Too many cooks, unlucky in love

A Partial Survey of Western European Holiday Migrations

for Trevor Winkfield

EXODUS A

Leeds' roads roam to all?
Rome's Leeds' road to all—
All Leeds rode to Rome.

EXODUS B

All Rome leads to roads.
Rome leads all to roads,
Leads Rome all to roads:
"Roam all leads to roads!"
Roads lead Rome to all?
All leads roam to Rhodes,
Lead all Rome to Rhodes.

RETURN A + B

Roads lead all to Rome,
Lead all Rhodes to Rome.
Rome-roads lead to all?
All roam roads to Leeds!
Rome rode all to Leeds.

SUMMARY

All roads roam to Leeds.

Jack's Reminders to the King of Karactika

Wait for no man.

Time and tide
wait for no man.

Stitches in time and tide
wait for no man.

Sticks and stones
    and stitches in time and tide
wait for no man.

Sticks and unturned stones
    and stitches in time and tide
wait for no man.

Sticks and unturned rolling stones
        and stitches in time and tide
wait for no man.

The things which are Caesar's
        and sticks and unturned rolling stones
        and stitches in time and tide
wait for no man.

What goes up
        and the things which are Caesar's
        and sticks and unturned rolling stones
        and stitches in time and tide
wait for no man.

Even breaks
        and what goes up
        and the things which are Caesar's
        and sticks and unturned rolling stones
        and stitches in time and tide
wait for no man.

Ill winds
     and even breaks
     and what goes up
     and the things which are Caesar's
     and sticks and unturned rolling stones
     and stitches in time and tide
wait for no man.

Roads to Rome
     and ill winds
     and even breaks
     and what goes up
     and the things which are Caesar's
     and sticks and unturned rolling stones
     and stitches in time and tide
wait for no man.

The road to Hell
      and the roads to Rome
      and ill winds
      and even breaks
      and what goes up
      and the things which are Caesar's
      and sticks and unturned rolling stones
      and stitches in time and tide
wait for no man.

All roads,
      the road to Hell
      and the roads to Rome,
      and ill winds
      and even breaks
      and what goes up
      and the things which are Caesar's
      and sticks and unturned rolling stones
      and stitches in time and tide
wait for no man.

Any port
      and all roads,
      the road to Hell
      and the roads to Rome,
      and ill winds and even breaks
      and what goes up
      and the things which are Caesar's
      and sticks and unturned rolling stones
      and stitches in time and tide
wait for no man.

Every cloud
      and any port
      and all roads,
      the road to Hell
      and the roads to Rome,
      and ill winds
      and even breaks
      and what goes up
      and the things which are Caesar's
      and sticks and unturned rolling stones
      and stitches in time and tide
wait for no man.

The west that is west
    and every cloud
    and any port
    and all roads,
    the road to Hell
    and the roads to Rome,
    and ill winds
    and even breaks
    and what goes up
    and the things which are Caesar's
    and sticks and unturned rolling stones
    and stitches in time and tide
wait for no man.

Red sky at night
    in the west that is west
    and every cloud
    and any port
    and all roads,
    the road to Hell
    and the roads to Rome,
    and ill winds
    and even breaks
    and what goes up
    and the things which are Caesar's
    and sticks and unturned rolling stones
    and stitches in time and tide
wait for no man.

The east that is east
  and red sky at night
  in the west that is west
  and every cloud
  and any port
  and all roads,
  the road to Hell
  and the roads to Rome,
  and ill winds
  and even breaks
  and what goes up
  and the things which are Caesar's
  and sticks and unturned rolling stones
  and stitches in time and tide
wait for no man.

Red sky at morning
    in the east that is east
    and red sky at night
    in the west that is west
    and every cloud
    and any port
    and all roads,
    the road to Hell
    and the roads to Rome,
    and ill winds
    and even breaks
    and what goes up
    and the things which are Caesar's
    and sticks and unturned rolling stones
    and stitches in time and tide

wait for no man.

HARRY MATHEWS

Born in New York City in 1930, Harry Mathews lives in America and France. From 1952 to 1978 he spent his years in Europe, involving himself with the French literary scene and becoming a member of the Ouvroir de littérature potentielle in Paris.

His books of poetry include *The Ring, Planisphere, Trial Impressions, La Savoir des rois, Armenian Papers: Poems 1954–1984,* and *Out of Bounds.* Among his works of fiction are *The Sinking of the Odradek Stadium, Tlooth, The Conversions, Cigarettes,* and *The Journalist,* winner of the 1994 America Award for Fiction. He was a recipient of a 1981 National Endowment for the Arts grant in fiction writing and in 1991 of an award for fiction from the American Academy and Institute of Arts and Letters.

ALEX KATZ

Born in Brooklyn, Alex Katz studied from 1945 to 1949 at the Cooper Union School of Art, and from 1949 through 1950 at the Skowhegan School of Paining and Sculpture, with which he is still associated. He has taught at Yale University School of Art (1961–63) and at the University of Pennsylvania School of Art (1971–72), and in 1972, he was awarded a Guggenheim Fellowship in painting. He has designed sets and costumes for the Paul Taylor Dance Company, and for Kenneth Koch's play *George Washington Crossing the Delaware.* He has also collaborated over the years with several poets and fiction writers, most notably John Ashbery, Kenneth Koch, and Harry Mathews.

SUN & MOON CLASSICS

EMMANUEL HOCQUARD [France]
The Cape of Good Hope [in preparation]

SIGURD HOEL [Norway]
The Road to the World's End 75 (1-55713-210-0, $13.95)

FANNY HOWE [USA]
The Deep North 15 (1-55713-105-8, $9.95)
Radical Love: A Trilogy [in preparation]
Saving History 27 (1-55713-100-7, $12.95)

SUSAN HOWE [USA]
The Europe of Trusts 7 (1-55713-009-4, $10.95)

LAURA (RIDING) JACKSON [USA]
Lives of Wives 71 (1-55713-182-1, $12.95)

HENRY JAMES [USA]
The Awkward Age [in preparation]
What Maisie Knew [in preparation]

LEN JENKIN [USA]
Dark Ride and Other Plays 22 (1-55713-073-6, $13.95)
Careless Love 54 (1-55713-168-6, $9.95)
Pilgrims of the Night: Five Plays [in preparation]

WILHELM JENSEN [Germany]
Gradiva 38 (1-55713-139-2, $13.95)

JEFFREY M. JONES [USA]
The Crazy Plays and Others [in preparation]
J. P. Morgan Saves the Nation 157 (1-55713-256-9, $9.95)
Love Trouble 78 (1-55713-198-8, $9.95)
Night Coil [in preparation]

SEVE KATZ [USA]
Florry of Washington Heights [in preparation]
43 Fictions 18 (1-55713-069-8, $12.95)
Swanny's Ways [in preparation]
Wier & Pouce [in preparation]

ALEXEI KRUCHENYKH [Russia]
Suicide Circus: Selected Poems [in preparation]

THOMAS LA FARGE [USA]
Terror of Earth [in preparation]

VALERY LARBAUD [France]
Childish Things 19 (1-55713-119-8, $13.95)

OSMAN LINS [Brazil]
Nine, Novena 104 (1-55713-229-1, $12.95)

NATHANIEL MACKEY [USA]
Bedouin Hornbook [in preparation]

JACKSON MAC LOW [USA]
Barnesbook [in preparation]
From Pearl Harbor Day to FDR's Birthday 126
   (0-940650-19-3, $10.95)
Pieces O' Six 17 (1-55713-060-4, $11.95)
Two Plays [in preparation]

CLARENCE MAJOR [USA]
Painted Turtle: Woman with Guitar (1-55713-085-x, $11.95)

F. T. MARINETTI [Italy]
Let's Murder the Moonshine: Selected Writings 12
   (1-55713-101-5, $13.95)
The Untameables 28 (1-55713-044-7, $10.95)

HARRY MATHEWS [USA]
Selected Declarations of Dependence (1-55713-234-8, $10.95)

FRIEDRIKE MAYRÖCKER [Austria]
with each clouded peak [in preparation]

DOUGLAS MESSERLI [USA]
After [in preparation]
Ed. *50: A Celebration of Sun & Moon Classics* 50
   (1-55713-132-5, $13.95)
Ed. *From the Other Side of the Century: A New American
   Poetry 1960–1990* 47 (1-55713-131-7, $29.95)
Ed. [with Mac Wellman] *From the Other Side of the
   Century II: A New American Drama 1960–1995* [in preparation]
River to Rivet: A Poetic Trilogy [in preparation]

DAVID MILLER [England]
The River of Marah [in preparation]

CHRISTOPHER MORLEY [USA]
Thunder on the Left 68 (1-55713-190-2, $12.95)

GÉRARD DE NERVAL [France]
Aurelia [in preparation]

VALÈRE NOVARINA [France]
The Theater of the Ears [in preparation]

CHARLES NORTH [USA]
New and Selected Poems [in preparation]

TOBY OLSON [USA]
Dorit in Lesbos [in preparation]
Utah [in preparation]

MAGGIE O'SULLIVAN [England]
Palace of Reptiles [in preparation]

SERGEI PARADJANOV [Armenia]
Seven Visions [in preparation]

ANTONIO PORTA [Italy]
Metropolis [in preparation]

ANTHONY POWELL [England]
Afternoon Men [in preparation]
Agents and Patients [in preparation]
From a View to a Death [in preparation]
O, How the Wheel Becomes It! 76 (1-55713-221-6, $10.95)
Venusburg [in preparation]
What's Become of Waring [in preparation]

SEXTUS PROPERTIUS [Ancient Rome]
Charm 89 (1-55713-224-0, $11.95)

RAYMOND QUENEAU [France]
Children of Clay [in preparation]

CARL RAKOSI [USA]
Poems 1923–1941 64 (1-55713-185-6, $12.95)

TOM RAWORTH [England]
Eternal Sections 23 (1-55713-129-5, $9.95)

NORBERTO LUIS ROMERO [Spain]
The Arrival of Autumn in Constantinople [in preparation]

MAC WELLMAN [USA]
 The Land Beyond the Forest: Dracula AND *Swoop* 112
  (1-55713-228-3, $12.95)
 The Land of Fog and Whistles: Selected Plays [in preparation]
 Two Plays: A Murder of Crows AND *The Hyacinth Macaw* 62
  (1-55713-197-X, $11.95)

JOHN WIENERS [USA]
 The Journal of John Wieners / is to be called [in preparation]

ÉMILE ZOLA [France]
 The Belly of Paris (1-55713-066-3, $14.95)

*

Individuals order from:
Sun & Moon Press
6026 Wilshire Boulevard
Los Angeles, California 90036
213-857-1115

Libraries and Bookstores in the United States and Canada
should order from:
Consortium Book Sales & Distribution
1045 Westgate Drive, Suite 90
Saint Paul, Minnesota 55114-1065
800-283-3572
FAX 612-221-0124

Libraries and Bookstores in the United Kingdom and on the Continent
should order from:
Password Books Ltd.
23 New Mount Street
Manchester M4 4DE, ENGLAND
0161 953 4009
INTERNATIONAL +44 61 953-4009
0161 953 4090